Murder by
A Pendle Witch Short Story

**Inspired by the True Story
of Jennet Preston**

Karen Perkins
LionheART Publishing House

First published in Great Britain in 2019 by
LionheART Publishing House

Copyright © Karen Perkins 2019, 2021
ISBN: 978-1-912842-38-4

This book is copyright under the Berne Convention
No reproduction without permission
All rights reserved.

The right of Karen Perkins to be identified as the author of this work has been asserted by her in accordance with sections 77 and 78 of the Copyright, Designs and Patents Act 1988.

LionheART Publishing House
Harrogate

lionheartpublishinghouse@gmail.com

This book is a work of fiction.
Whilst based on historical events, names, characters and incidents are either a product of the author's imagination or are used fictitiously.

Author's Note

To reflect the setting and characters of 17th-century Yorkshire, a flavour of the Yorkshire dialect is used in the dialogue and narrative, for example:

Allus (always)
Hersen/Hissen/Mesen (herself/himself/myself)
Mebbe (maybe)
Nithering (cold)
Nowt (nothing)
Reet (right)
Summat (something)

Hie, Grim, come thee here
Great beast dispel my fear
Send the witches down to Hell
Help me now and toll the bell

– Old English charm against witches

Murder by Witchcraft
A Pendle Witch Short Story

Inspired by the True Story of Jennet Preston

Chapter 1

Late April 1612

I stumbled forward into a familiar gloomy stench at his push. The heavy, iron-bound oak door slammed behind me and I heard the mechanism of the lock as York Castle's gaoler secured his dungeon. I stood where I were, frozen in disbelief. How could I be back here mere weeks after Sir Edward Bromley and his jury freed me?

I shivered and pulled my cloak around me as I peered into the gloom, trying to pick out the deeper shadows of figures.

It were nithering in here. As it had been before. But how many others would I be sharing this place with this time? And who were they? What had they done to be kept in here months ahead of the next Assizes? It had to be summat serious, otherwise they'd have had bail. The gaoler were fond of coin.

'Are you just going to stand there?'

I recognised the voice. 'John Wilson? That cannot be you still here.'

'Aye, lass, here I still be.' His words were broken off by deep coughing.

I took a tentative step forward then shuddered at a splash and an icy chill seeping into my stockings. The stink of stagnant water and shite slapped me, and I gasped, slapping my hand over my mouth and nose.

Wilson chuckled, a strange sound in these environs. 'Aye, still flooded. Reckon you've missed worst of it, though.'

The gloom seemed to lift as my eyes grew used to it, and I moved by instinct. John's voice came from the same corner he'd occupied earlier in the month, and I took small steps forward, skirts raised out of the mire, resigned to the smell and the scurrying of fleeing rodents. Then I remembered my last incarceration here and let my skirts fall. There were no point in trying to keep them dry.

The pool of water were not as large as I remembered, and I rose out of it as I moved further away from the wall bounded by the River Foss. I sat, doing my best not to think about what I were sitting in. From memory, no part of this stone floor would be anything approaching clean. 'I'd understood you to be freed, John, as I were.'

'Aye. Not guilty of coining. The main evidence in my favour being that I have no coin.'

'Not usually a good thing,' I remarked as I shuffled closer to share some warmth. Old habits never left us it seemed.

'And not so now.' John gave that strange, high-pitched chuckle once more. 'I've no coin to pay my fees, nor family to settle my debt for me.'

'So they *keep* you here?'

'Aye. Not guilty I may be, but I'll not see freedom until I find some coin.'

'How much do you owe?' William had settled my own debt to the gaoler and had not told me the amount. Just how much had my husband paid my tormentors?

'Nine shillings,' Wilson said.

'But that's a full month's wages!'

'Aye. And I'll die in here for it.' He chuckled once more.

'Turned him mad, it has. Forever laughing,' a woman said.

'Better than the screaming and raging he put us all through at first,' another said.

'True enough. Once the gaoler started adding shilling fines to his debt every time he cursed him or the judge, castle or court, he's found a comfort in mirth.'

'There's some sense in that,' I allowed, trying to imagine the joyful relief on release being slaughtered by the horror of continued incarceration in this place, with no end in sight. Happen I'd choose madness too in them circumstances.

'I'm Maggie Thorne,' the first woman said.

'Lizzie Nixon,' said the second.

'Jennet Preston,' I completed the trilogy of introductions.

'Ahh, the witch,' Maggie said. 'We've been hearing about you. Aye, and them others an'all.'

I bridled. 'I ain't no witch! I were tried for it once before and the good jurymen declared me innocent.'

'Then why are you here again if you ain't no witch?'

'If I were a witch, do you not think I'd have flown somewhere far away from this place?'

'She makes a good point there,' Lizzie said.

'But them other witches, them she kens ower Pendle way, word is they were planning to blow up Lancaster Castle, just like Gunpowder Treason.'

'Aye, that's right,' a man's voice joined the discussion. 'I heard about that. I reckon they were planning to blow up York Castle, an'all. Is that why you're here and not off with the Devil?'

I could barely see him, but recognised the movements of his right arm. He'd crossed hissen. A priest then. Another Catholic in this hellhole. I couldn't decide if that were a good thing or nay.

Then the full import of his words hit me and I took a breath, terrified by what they were saying, then coughed and retched on the foul stench of fetid water and human waste.

'Nonsense,' I croaked, when I could speak once more. 'Thomas Lister. *He's* why I'm here. There's no plots nor witches. Just a man lost in grief and hatred.'

'But Lister's a fine gentleman, why would he bother himself with the likes of you?' the priest asked.

'I knew his father. He thinks I knew him too well.'

'Ahh,' the women said in understanding. 'And did you?'

My breath hitched as I remembered just in time to avoid drawing in a great chestful of air. 'He were my master, nowt more.'

'You're the one that murdered him,' Lizzie exclaimed. 'They say he bled when you touched his corpse!'

'Nowt but malicious gossip.' I waved the absurd accusation away.

'Aye, damnable gossip. Put us all in here it has, eh, Lizzie?' Maggie elbowed her friend.

'I had nowt to do with his father's death, nor that of his mam, neither,' I protested.

'Aye, we know, just like we had nowt to do with counterfeit coins at Thursday market, and Father Greaves here ain't no priest.'

'That's right, Lizzie, he ain't no priest, and them bad guineas were nowt to do with us, neither.' Maggie giggled. 'All of us are as innocent as Mad John here.'

'But—' I stopped short: fear, anger and despair taking the words from my tongue. 'I've done nowt,' I whispered, to another chuckle and cough from John Wilson. No bugger else heard me.

Chapter 2

The door crashed against the wall, startling us all, and eliciting at least one cry of surprise. Happen it were Lizzie, although it could just as easily have been an exclamation from John Wilson.

I jumped to my feet and stared at the man who filled the doorway, cudgel in one hand and manacles in the other. This were no routine interruption to our misery for weevil-infested bread, mouldy cheese and stale small ale.

'Jennet Preston,' he said. 'Get yoursen ower here.' He held the manacles high.

My knees almost gave way, and I rested against the wall for a moment before I could make my way through the puddles to the door.

'Witch has spelled hersen a visitor,' Maggie whispered to Lizzie.

'She could have thought to bring my Jack while she were at it,' Lizzie complained. 'He still ain't come.'

'He won't come, Lizzie. Scared of getting locked up hissen, ain't he?'

I ignored them both, but could not resist aiming my step to splash putrid water at Father Greaves crossing hissen as I moved past.

I held out my hands, wrist to wrist, remembering the routine, and he pushed the iron shackles around them, which he then threaded on to a short iron bar. He snapped the lock into place, but I did not give my gaoler the satisfaction of a wince. Working for the Lister family for so many years had schooled me well, and I could hide all but the worst pain.

The gaoler gave me a shove with his cudgel and I stumbled forward, striking my shoulder against the uneven stone wall of the passage. I grunted but lurched upright once more and stepped forward towards the light.

A rusted iron gate blocked my path, and my heart raced as I breathed in fresh air. I filled my chest despite the gaoler pushing me aside to unlock the gate. On the other side, I waited again for him to secure it behind us, then struggle to unlock the next. Rust flaked away as he scraped it against the stone to push it aside.

'In there.' He opened a heavy door, released my manacles, then pushed me backwards inside a room flooded with light.

It took me some moments to gather my wits, and I felt arms about me, holding me, crushing me. I turned within his embrace. 'William!'

When at last I persuaded him to release me, he led me to a bench next to a board laden with food. My mouth watered and I grabbed bread, cheese, and proper ale.

'That's Old Man Hodgeson's best ale,' my husband said. 'And Peggy sent some of her butter, and that's Alf's honey, and Mary's cheese. And here's one of Betty's mutton pies.' He pulled the pie out of his sack and presented it to me in triumph. 'The whole village is up in arms about you being arrested again. Lister hardly leaves his manor house except with a guard of four.' He paused to watch me eat. 'I'm sorry it took me so long to come. I didn't know they'd taken you here till yesterday. Thought Nowell still had you at Read Hall. The bastard never told us he committed you here last week.'

I looked up at him. 'A week? Have I been here only a week?' Unbidden, a tear rolled down my cheek. I had thought it nearer a month. How could it be a mere week? I stared at William, saw the new lines etched on his face, the way he'd aged even further since I last saw him. I dared not think about what he saw as he met my gaze.

'Aye, it is, love.'

I dropped the wedge of cheese I'd been gnawing on, my appetite dulled. 'Oh William, I cannot do this again, not again.'

'Aye, thee can, love. You'll do this, and you'll come home again. But you stay away from Pendle this time!'

'I were only trying to help.'

'I know, love. But look where it's got you. And rest of 'em an'all.'

'Rest of 'em, what do you mean?'

William looked shocked. 'Don't you know?'

'Well, I knew summat were going on when Nowell and Bannester turned up with young James Device that day and took me to Read Hall, but they've told me nowt, just as I told them nowt.'

William sighed and rubbed his whiskers. 'You'd best have some more ale.' He passed me the jug.

Chapter 3

'They're all at Lancaster Castle? *All* of 'em? Even little 'uns?'

'Most of 'em, half a dozen fled, but them we know best are at Lancaster, although I heard Little Jennet Device is still at Read Hall. Mebbe James too, none know for sure.'

'But they've done nowt! *None* of us did owt!'

'That's not what they say, love. There's talk of Black Sabbats, naming of spirits, and the use of clay pictures and teeth robbed from graves to curse folk.'

'What?' I couldn't believe my ears. 'We talked about the four already in Lancaster Castle – Alizon Device, her grandmother Demdike, Chattox and Anne Redferne – that's all. Their families and friends wanted to know how things were for me, and what I said at trial to be released.'

'There's also talk of feasting and slaughtering a lamb. On Good Friday.'

I didn't speak for a moment. 'We did have meat, aye, but mutton not lamb, although there were plenty of ale too. We were celebrating my freedom, and toasting them still held.'

'But Good Friday, Jennet!'

'We never thought owt about it. Too busy worrying about their kin.'

'So nobody suggested killing Lancaster's gaoler and blowing up castle?'

I stared at him. Father Greaves had mentioned summat like that. I'd thought nay more about it, but how had William heard same tales?

'Please tell me you never asked for help to curse Thomas Lister and his uncle.'

I said nowt.

'Jennet?' His brow creased into a frown.

'Only in jest. None of 'em took me as serious.'

'It seems young James and Jennet Device did. And happy to tell Nowell and Bannester all about it an'all. Oh Jennet, what have you done?'

'Nowt! I've done nowt! Had a feast of meat and ale three days after getting home from this damned gaol, and making light of what happened. We all laugh at danger and worries, 'tis only way to find strength to meet 'em at times. Tell me I'm wrong!'

William said nowt, just stared at me, his frown growing fiercer.

'Oh, William.' I fell against him once more. 'Is he gonna win, will Lister get his way after all?'

William tightened his arms around me. 'Not if I can help it, love.'

'Why does he hate me so much? I've done nowt but serve him, and his mam and father afore him. And I kept me mouth shut an'all. There's plenty I could have said about his father, but I didn't, you know I didn't.'

'Aye, I do, love. An' he hates you as he cannot think ill of his father. If he can't think ill of his father, then he'll hear his father's dying words as an accusation, not a confession. And now he has Nowell and Bannester stirring his hatred yet further.'

I jumped as the door slammed open.

'Five minutes more,' William said, pushing me aside and rising to stand before the gaoler. I spotted the glint of coin changing hands, and the man turned about and left us.

'You cannot be throwing coin away like that, William, we have little enough as it is.'

'Don't fret, love. Whole of Gisborne came together and found enough coin for this, and to buy you a bed for a sennight. We'll do what we need to when we need more.'

'Nay, William, it's tuppence a night for a bed. Keep the money, and raise as much as you can. If what you say about Roger Nowell and Nicholas Bannester joining Lister is true, we may have more urgent need of it than for the rent of a stinking, lice-ridden bed.'

'We'll be reet, love. If Fortune favours us, you'll be before Sir Bromley again, and not t'other one.'

'Which other one?'

William dropped his gaze and my blood chilled. 'Sir James Altham.'

'But he's Bannester's man! Altham won't go against Bannester, not that toad!'

William had no words, and my own slipped away. I leaned against him, savouring the feel of his renewed and quiet embrace while I could.

The silence were again broken by the slamming of the door.

While William made further protest, I gathered the remaining food from the boards, and thrust it into the sack. There were enough for all my new acquaintances. Even Father Greaves. I needed all the friends I could find.

And I'd likely have need of a priest before long an'all.

Chapter 4

May 1612

I jumped as the door crashed open. We all watched the gaoler, wondering whose name he would call. Had William returned? Or had Lizzie's Jack finally come to visit?

'Jennet Preston. Here.'

My heart soared as he pressed the manacles over my wrists and locked them into place. *William's here.*

'Don't forget to bring food back!' Maggie called out and I nodded at her with a large smile. Life within this terrible place had grown easier after I shared the food from William's last visit. Now I had friends here.

I turned towards the light, enjoying the feel of it on my face – even though it were considerably weakened – but the gaoler shoved me in the opposite direction.

'What is it? Where are you taking me?'

The gaoler said nowt, but used his cudgel to prod me towards a door set into the dark, dank passage.

He opened it and pushed me inside.

Three men sat at a board laden with meat and jugs of ale, but I could only smell the River Foss on the other side of the stone wall behind them. It seemed a sham of William's visit, and I wondered if they'd purposely recreated the scene.

The gaoler pushed me on to a small stool. I raised my hands to have the manacles removed, but he only moved behind me to stand before the door.

My heart sank as I regarded the three men. I knew them all. Thomas Lister: the man who'd devised all my woes. Thomas Heber: the magistrate who'd failed to convince the Lent Assizes of any guilt on my behalf. And Roger Nowell: the Lancashire witch hunter who'd had me at his mercy at Read Hall less than a month before, and who'd pursued so many of my Pendle friends to the gaol at Lancaster.

All three were dressed in their finery and I spared a thought for the poor washerwomen who would be tasked with removing the grime and stench of this gaol from their fine padded doublets, woollen hose and linen shirts; even the imposing, tall-crowned hats remained atop their heads in defiance of good manners.

'Are you hungry, Mistress Preston?' Roger Nowell indicated the spread before him with an inviting hand.

I said nowt. I already knew his tricks. I hoped I would not be learning more this day.

'Answer our questions and you can eat and drink your fill.' Nowell picked up one of the jugs and poured some of the contents into a goblet. The liquid were red. Wine, then, not ale. Despite mesen, my eyes fixed on the goblet, and I could not move them away.

Thomas Lister reached over to a roasted bird. Peahen or goose, I could not tell from this far distant. He pulled a leg from the carcass and the smell of its flesh flooded my nose. My mouth watered, and I could tell by his smile that he knew it.

I said nowt.

'You may even be allowed to go home, and live out your days with your husband.'

I jerked my eyes to Nowell's and stared at him in shock. Could he really mean that? He smiled, and my guts churned.

'First things first,' Lister said, and the disturbance in my guts grew ever more violent. He had no intention of allowing me to return to Gisborne. 'Confess to your witching of my father.'

I said nowt.

He pointed the leg of meat at me and raised his eyebrows.

Hunger and fear combined to make me nauseous and my mouth flooded with moisture. I swallowed it down, determined not to show my terror to these men.

'Tell us of the pact you made with the Devil!' Lister

roared, leaping to his feet. 'Confess to the murder of my father!'

Heber reached out a hand to Lister's forearm, and the young man took a deep breath, sat, nodded and took the goblet of wine for himself.

Roger Nowell cleared his throat. 'Let us begin afresh,' he said. 'What is the form of your familiar?'

I said nowt.

'Did you use any of Thomas Lister's clothing to curse him after you'd done away with his father?'

Surprise forced the word out of me. 'No!' What were he talking about?

'What did you do to cause Thomas Lister his recent great losses?'

'What losses?' I said, then regretted my words as Nowell smiled. I knew how this would go. I were reminded of my first days at Read Hall, where Nowell had forced me to change my clothes – before him and two of his retainers. The woman had shaved every part of me in her examinations, and he had asked me questions like this. Although then he had been asking about the Devices, Chattox and others who lived in or about Pendle. My blood ran cold and I shivered, wondering what he would do to me today.

'Did you repair to Demdike's abode, Malkin Tower, to ask her kin for aid in cursing Thomas Lister here and his uncle, Leonard Lister?'

I said nowt.

'Come, woman.' Heber slammed his fist on the

board. 'Answer these questions and you may eat!'

I didn't believe him, and cursed my belly for its groanings, which I knew the men heard.

'If you don't confess, perjury will be added to your list of crimes,' Nowell said with a chiding glance at Heber, who poured himself a goblet of wine.

I stared at him and said nowt.

Lister sighed in impatience. 'This is getting us nowhere. We must undertake the usual interrogations for a witch. Do you have your pricker?'

I could not help my gasp of fear.

Nowell stared at me a moment longer, then turned to Lister. 'She has already been pricked, at Read Hall, and no mark was found. I also had her watched for two days and nights, and no imp or familiar was spotted.'

My mind cast back to the watching. He had tied me to a chair, where I'd stayed for two days and nights, with little food or ale, forced to soil mesen where I sat. Every time my eyes closed, to try to escape the torture, I were forced to waken. When they had finally set me free, I had been unable to straighten my legs, and it had been hours until I were able to stand once more. Then they had brought me here.

'Then we must take the next steps,' Lister said with a frown.

'Which are?' Heber asked as he leaned forward to cut a slice of meat from the haunch of mutton before him.

'Penne forte et dure.'

What?

'Pressing?' Heber asked. 'Surely that will not be necessary.'

I said nowt, although I had to force my lips against the pleas for mercy that wanted to escape. The thought of being pressed . . . Being forced to lie on a stone floor, having a door laid ower me, having that door weighted down with boulders until my poor body . . . I could not finish the thought. Surely they would not go so far?

'Gentlemen, there must be another way,' Heber protested.

'Witchcraft is high treason against God's Majesty,' Lister said, and I hated him in that moment more than I had ever thought possible. 'And as such, torture is wholly justified.'

I made to stand; all I wanted were to hurt him, aye, even to kill him. The gaoler's hands pushed me down before I had even halfway risen.

'But not if it kills her, crushes her to death, and she still does not confess,' Heber persisted. ' 'Tis akin to murder then!'

'We shall not press her,' Nowell said. 'I need her alive. Her conviction is important not only for these Assizes, but for the forthcoming trials in Lancaster.'

'Then what?' Lister said, disgust evident in his voice. 'With all your tricks you have not yet secured any confession – neither here nor when you had her at Read Hall!'

Nowell ignored him, then nodded at the gaoler behind me. I watched the man approach and place something from his scrip upon the table. I could not see what it were.

He moved back to his previous position before the door.

Roger Nowell picked up the object, and I realised that in fact there were two of the iron implements.

I watched in dawning horror as he held up the first one so I could clearly see the three prongs. It were a thumbikin. He turned the butterfly screw on the central prong until it were near the top, then raised the iron plate beneath it. Every movement were slow and deliberate. He ensured that he had not only my full attention, but Lister and Heber's too.

He stood and nodded to the gaoler, and I soon felt the man's hands on my shoulders, his belly behind my back, pressing me down to the stool despite my desperate squirming.

Nowell pushed my left thumb into the gap between the left and central prong of the device, and Lister helped him place my right thumb to the other side of the central screw. I had not even noticed him rise from his seat.

I were trapped, the gaoler using his weight to keep me in place on the chair. Manacles were holding my wrists flush together. And now Nowell reversed the butterfly screw, tightening it, pushing the iron bar down on to my thumbs, and pressing my thumbs against the second bar below.

I gasped in pain as the bars pressed into my flesh,

and gritted my teeth, forcing my mind to focus on William, doing everything I could to block out what were happening here.

'Is your familiar a white foal?'

I said nowt, and he tightened the thumbscrew further. This time my gasp became a small scream, as I felt the pressure on my bones.

'Did you seek vengeance on Master Lister for his prosecution of you for murdering the Dodgeson child?'

'No!' I screamed, desperately trying to keep a picture of William's face in my mind, as Nowell tightened the thumbscrew until I heard – and felt – the cracks.

Nowell returned to the table to fetch the second thumbikin.

He looked down at my feet.

I curled my toes as I cried out, 'No!' Now that I had screamed once, I could not stop, and shriek after shriek rent the air. William's face faded from my mind to be replaced by a gradual darkening.

'Enough,' I heard Heber say. 'That's enough.'

'She has clearly bewitched herself into keeping her confession silent.' That were Lister's voice.

Innocent I came to gaol, innocent I am tortured. Innocent I shall die. But I could not push the words out past my screams, and I finally slipped into a welcome, freezing nothingness.

Chapter 5

July 1612

'Can you not do something about your man there?'

I turned to glare at the woman. She'd come in a fortnight since with her husband. As far as I could tell, their only crime were to be gypsies. No matter, I were not giving up my spot by the narrow slit in the wall. I were up to my ankles in filthy water, my thumbs still pained me, and I stood hunched up to protect them under my arms. The smell from the Foss on the other side of the wall were none too fresh, but it were a damn sight better than the stink in this place.

It had been bad enough when I arrived, but now there must be four dozen folk in here. Men and women, even children, with crimes ranging from publishing unlawful books or being a seminary priest to coining, piracy or, of course, murder by witchcraft.

They'd come from all ower Yorkshire. I mesen from Gisborne were closest to County of Lancaster int' west, and the pirate were from Scarborough o'course. There were folk from Hull, Bradford and

Knaresborough, and a fair showing of York folk too. And the gypsies o'course. Lord knew where they were from.

John Wilson suffered another coughing fit and I sighed, motioned the gypsy woman to take my place and find a little fresher air, and limped my way through sprawled limbs, drowned rats and clutching fingers to tend to him.

He grabbed my hand as I seated mesen next to him, and I winced at the warmth of his skin, and the crawling sensation I had whenever he touched me. 'How do, John?'

His only response were laughter. A high-pitched cackle now. I had not thought I would miss the chuckle with which he'd first greeted me on my return to this dungeon.

I gritted my teeth and pushed aside the ties of his shirt to peer at his chest. The red spots of gaol fever were barely there, but I did not doubt that they would grow. But there were nowt I could do for him. I sat back and scratched at my arm. Looking about me I wondered how many more were festering death. Were the heat in me own skin from the same cause, or summat else?

Surely it could not be much longer till we left this hellhole.

* * *

The door banged open in the gaoler's usual fashion and I stiffened when I saw that this time he had a guard of half a dozen with him, all bearing arms. It were time then. Suddenly I were not so keen to leave this pit.

He called near twenty names, including Maggie Thorne and Lizzie Nixon. Both women held their hands out to me and I grasped them with care, the fear in their eyes no doubt reflected in my own, and none of us finding any words. But none were needed. We all felt the same, and no words had been created to aid us in this fetid mixture of terror, hope and futility.

They were pulled away and I were left holding nowt but air.

Father Greaves took my arm. 'Come,' he said, and led me back to John Wilson.

We sat by the suffering man, and others joined us. I noticed the pirate, the other priest, and men charged with robbery and murder. All the serious crimes. The hanging crimes.

I were not the only woman, though – the gypsy woman were still here with her husband, as well as another two accused of witchcraft.

We gathered together, now happy to have the comfort of others close by, and keeping out of the worst of the flooding.

Father Greaves led the prayers, and none bothered about Protestant or Catholic. It were just good to have the comfort of a man of God.

Then our names were all called. All but John Wilson's. I reached over to him to bid my farewell, and he gave me a weak smile. 'God be with you, Jennet,' he whispered.

'Ain't no God in this place,' I muttered, too quiet for the priests to hear.

Chapter 6

27th July 1612

We were taken to the chapel abutting the gaol. Bowls of cold but fairly clear water were lined up on a long trestle and we were pushed towards them. I'm sure the gesture were more for the sensibilities of the court than for our own comfort.

After we'd washed, we were manacled once more and forced into the front benches. The Chaplain of the Castle awaited us, and I noted the pulpit were fair distant from our seats. So he were frit of gaol fever an'all.

I paid no attention to his admonishments nor his sermoning. I closed my eyes and thought of William. The life we had. The life we could have had, should events have taken a different course.

A name were called, and I opened my eyes to see the Scarborough pirate stand and follow the gaoler. The courthouse were next door, I knew from my last visit. I supposed it were a Protestant vanity, having the chapel betwixt dungeon and courthouse. Their own idea of Purgatory as their religion allowed for none in the next world.

I shut my eyes once more. This were my time, they'd already taken more than enough from me, I'd lose mesen in every moment of dreams I could.

'Jennet Preston.'

I opened my eyes. My heart sank as I took in the bare, whitewashed walls and the stark trestle bearing a plain wooden cross in place of a proper altar and crucifix. If ever there were a time to see my saviour at the moment of his martyrdom, it were now. But he were not here, not in this castle of the Protestant Scottish king.

'*Jennet Preston!*'

I stood as my manacles were grasped and wrenched upwards, forced my feet to move towards my persecutor, then looked him in the eye. It were the same man who'd called me three months past when I'd first faced this court on a similar charge. He could not hold my gaze.

At least that were one triumph I could take from this day.

The courtroom fell silent as I entered, and I were pleased to note some familiar faces amongst the observers sat on the dark oak benches that made up the gallery. Many of my neighbours had made the journey across the County of York, and I cast my eyes about the crowded room to find William's. He smiled and nodded towards me and I took strength from his presence. Then I turned to face the judges' bench and my heart sank.

Sir Edward Bromley were sat there, sure enough, but not at the centre. That position were taken by Sir James Altham, and on his other side were the Lancashire witch hunters, Roger Nowell and Nicholas Bannester.

I twisted to catch William's eye once more, but instead my eyes lit on those of young Thomas Lister. He smirked at me as I were persuaded forward by the gaoler who removed the manacles. I rubbed my wrists and took my place before the barre.

Altham flicked a finger at the prosecuting magistrate, Thomas Heber – the same man who had failed in his task to have me hanged only three months prior, and who had since partaken of my torture. He rose to his feet and gave me a distasteful glance. He bowed to the bench, then spoke.

'Your Honour, it is with great sadness and concern that I must outline to you the wicked and felonious deeds carried out by this woman, Jennet Preston.'

He flung out an arm to point at me on his last word, and I met his gaze, refusing to look away. We both knew he had uttered this phrase once before, almost word for word. He turned his attention back to the jury.

'I shall present to you examinations and witnesses to show you that this woman has feloniously practised, used and exercised diverse wicked and devilish arts, called witchcrafts, enchantments, charms and sorceries in and upon one Thomas Lister Esquire of Westby in Craven, in the County of York, and by force of the same witchcraft she feloniously killed the said Thomas Lister Senior four years since.'

Altham nodded, then looked at me. I stood firm as his eyes ran up and down me, though could not stop my hands twitching. 'And what do you plead to this despicable charge?'

'As my Lord God knows, I am innocent,' I said, my voice steady. 'I once more put mesen in His keeping.'

Altham stared at me a moment, then nodded to a gentleman standing at the back of the room. 'Master Sheriff, you may return your jury to hear this matter.'

'Your Honour,' the sheriff acknowledged, then opened the door to admit and swear in the twelve men who'd been waiting in the Grand Jury House.

Once the court had settled, Heber stood once more to describe his case to the jurymen.

Chapter 7

Pain shot through my jaw, yet I could not loosen it, even though it felt like my teeth would crumble from the force in it. The claims this man were making were beyond madness, yet he seemed to believe every word he were saying. And Altham and the jurymen were nodding along with his discourse as if it were a reasonable account of events.

'And now, I shall call Anne Robinson to describe to you the events on the night of Thomas Lister's death, which also happened to be the night of his son's wedding.'

Aye, his wedding to your daughter. My jaw clenched even tighter. Protesting would do me no good at this juncture. I had to keep the words inside, and not anger the judges or jurymen.

Young Thomas Lister hissen escorted Annie to the front of the courtroom to stand before the judges and jurymen. I glared at him as he made his way past me back to his seat. He all but smirked in return. My hands clenched into fists.

I turned my attention to Annie as Heber had her swear on the new King James' Bible that she would tell the truth this day. Ha, that flit of a girl wouldn't know the truth if she stared at it a week long.

'Aye, that's right,' she were saying. 'I were at your hall at Bracewell, sir, on the occasion of the marriage of your daughter Jane to the young master there.' She nodded towards Thomas Lister, but had not yet met my eye. 'There to help with the preparation and serving of the wedding feast and assist throughout the celebrations.'

'And how did those celebrations proceed?' Heber asked.

'Well enough at start,' Annie acknowledged, 'but things took a turn in the evening.'

'A turn, you say?'

'Aye sir.'

'Come, come, my girl,' Judge Altham butted in. 'We'll have no more of this hesitancy. You have sworn on the good book that you shall tell us the truth of this matter, and tell us you will.' He glared at Annie, who looked like a frit hare who'd spotted the fox.

Now she met my eye, her face reddened and I recognised the fear she held. So she had no choice but to do this. No matter, I would not encourage her to condemn me. I stared at her, daring her to turn and run from this court.

She flinched and looked past me to Lister, then drew her shoulders back and turned her gaze on Altham. 'I beg your pardon, Your Honour, this is all . . .' She did not finish her sentence, but waved her hand at the crowded courtroom.

'Yes, yes, but you must tell us what you witnessed on the night of the seventh of February in the year of our Lord, 1607,' Heber said, then softened his voice. 'Just tell Sir Altham and Sir Bromley what you told me.'

Annie nodded and watched her fingers twisting knots as she considered her next words. 'Well, as I say, it were the young master's wedding, and we were at Bracewell Hall. We'd just cleared away the plates and were moving trestles back to make room for the dancing, when Master Lister's father, well, he were took strange, he were.'

'What do you mean by strange?' Heber prompted.

'Well, he fell down and just lay there, twitching and thumping his legs an' head against floor. And he were screaming fit to wake dead. Terrifying to watch, it were.

'Anyroad, everyone stopped what they were doing, and the young master rushed to his father. My John and a couple of others helped lift the master on to a settle, and put a pillow under his head. His arms and legs were still kicking like a bad-tempered mule's, sir. Well, you know, you saw it an' all.'

'We're just interested in what you saw, Mistress Robinson.'

'Begging your pardon, Your Honour. Well, there were a reet to-do, no one knew what were happening.

Some even wondered if it were poison, you know as he were took ill after feasting, like, but no one else were taken badly, so we didn't reckon it could be poison, otherwise everyone would have been taken badly, wouldn't they? Stands to reason that does.'

My lips stretched in a small smile. *That's reet, Annie, you gabble on like that, it can only help me, that can.*

'What did you see and hear, Mistress Robinson?' I scowled as Heber interrupted her stream of words.

'Oh aye, well we didn't see no poison that's for sure.'

'But what *did* you see? What did you hear?'

'Oh, reet, that, aye, well . . .' The observers behind me tittered as Annie, flustered, tried to compose herself. 'Reet, well, it were uproar it were, one minute the young master and his bride were preparing to dance, the next, his father's insensible ont' settle and looking possessed.'

'Possessed?' Altham asked.

'Aye, Your Honour, possessed by Devil or one of his minions. Or bewitched.' She glanced at me, then looked back towards the bench. 'His face were pulled into such a show of fear and terror, and his body jerking all ower t'place, it were evil it were, could be nowt else but Devil.'

'Or someone who had called on Him,' Heber added.

'Aye, reet enough, sir. And then, then . . . with the mistress reet next to him trying to calm him, that's when he said it.' She looked at Heber triumphantly, then cast her gaze around the courtroom.

'Said what, Mistress Robinson?' Altham prompted with a sigh of exasperation. 'What did Master Lister say?'

'Oh, reet, aye, well, he said . . .' She paused to add import to her words, but I could not smile at her antics now, she were damning me with her mummers' ways.

Altham raised an eyebrow.

'He said her name. Jennet Preston.' She pointed at me. 'With his dying breath, he cried out, "Jennet Preston lays heavy upon me, Preston's wife lays heavy upon me, help me, help me," and then he left this life.'

'So,' Heber said, raising a hand to stop Annie continuing. 'Lying in great extremity upon his death bed, Thomas Lister accused this woman, Jennet Preston, of his own murder?'

'Aye sir,' Annie said, and I could restrain mesen no longer.

'Nay, nay, he were not accusing me, he were confessing his guilt of how he were to me. He were asking for forgiveness, from me, from his wife, and aye, from my husband an'all.'

'Silence!' Sir Altham roared. 'It is not your place to speak!'

'But he'd done me wrong, tried to force hissen on me, and it were his guilt that lay heavy on him!'

'Master Bailiff!'

I gasped as the bailiff approached. I had no wish to be gagged. 'I beg your pardon, Your Honour.'

'The prisoner at the barre shall not speak again until invited to do so.'

I bowed my head in reluctant acceptance, and Altham waved the bailiff back to his position.

'Master Heber, pray continue your examination of this witness.'

'Your Honour.' Heber bowed, then turned to face Annie once more. 'So Master Lister called out Jennet Preston's name with his dying breath. What happened next?'

'Well, we were laying him out, and all the household came to pay their last respects, and then *she* came.'

'By she, you mean Jennet Preston?'

'Aye sir. She came to him when he were in his winding sheet, and before God as my witness, when she touched his dead corpse, it bled afresh.'

A gasp filled the courtroom and I stared at Annie in shock. It were not true. He had not bled at my touch, it were nowt but a stain already there ont' linen!

'His corpse bled afresh at her touch?' Heber repeated the accusation that were the most damning proof of a murderer's guilt.

'Aye sir.'

'You are sure of this?'

Annie glanced at her young master, then repeated,

'Aye sir. And Master Lister and a fair few others saw it too.'

I did not need to turn to know that Lister nodded his agreement. I became aware in the hush that my fists were clenched tight enough to draw blood, and I hid my hands in the folds of my skirts so no one would think my fresh blood were confirmation of Lister's lies. For it were Lister, I were sure of it. Annie had always had a soft spot for him, ever since he were a nipper, and she were not the quickest of folk. He wouldn't have needed the five full years between then and now to persuade her that she saw fresh blood that day.

Chapter 8

'Now, Mistress Preston, you may speak. You have heard the wicked indictments against you, you have heard the account of Mistress Anne Robinson, plus that of Master Thomas Lister, who confirmed everything she said of you. Now do you confess your guilt?'

'I do not, Your Honour.' My voice broke on the last word. Honour were not a virtue present in this courtroom. 'I did not murder Master Lister. I have murdered no man, woman, nor child.' I directed this last at Sir Bromley, who met my eye. I kept my gaze on him as I defended mesen.

'I live in the parish of Gisborne, and both I and my husband have been in service to the Lister family at Westby for many years. The old master had a special liking for me—'

'Lies, I tell you!' The young Lister were on his feet, and shouted down by my kin.

'Master Lister,' Altham cautioned, and he retook his seat.

'A few months afore he died, the master suffered a seizure similar to the one described in this courtroom today, although it were not so severe. I helped him into his bed to rest, but he pulled at me with great strength, muttering such threats as to what he would do to me, what he had allus wanted to do to me.' I stopped, embarrassed to have to repeat this.

'It were not like him, and I cried out. I thought he would force me, on my honour.' I held Bromley's eye. 'My husband came and helped me away from him. This were unusual behaviour for Master Lister, as he had never before tried to force me, and I can but assume it were an effect of his sickness. He came to me a few days later when he were well again to beg my pardon, and I could tell he were fair worried about what had happened. It laid heavy on him – he used them words, I swear it.'

'Did anyone else witness these events?' Heber asked.

'Nay sir, I were alone with him until my husband came, but he can tell you same.'

'A husband does not make a good witness, Mistress, not in matters of this import against a wife.'

'Indeed,' came a voice from the gallery. My teeth clenched as I recognised Lister's tone.

Altham banged his gavel for silence and Heber continued. 'That does not explain the bleeding of the corpse.'

' 'Tis a falsehood, Your Honour. Master Lister did not bleed after his death. The young master would rather believe in the innocence of his father than in mine. His emotions were high as it were his wedding day, and his mother were also sore distressed, and stayed so until the day she died. 'Tis his grief which has forged this falsehood, and he has brought others into it.'

I glared at Master Heber.

'Your Honour!' Heber jumped to his feet in protest.

'You are the man's father-in-law!' I shouted. 'Lister often dines at your table, and yours, sir, and yours!' I pointed at Roger Nowell and Nicholas Bannester sitting alongside the judges.

'Silence!' Altham roared and once more banged his gavel. 'I will not have this court maligned!'

I took a deep breath to calm mesen, then turned to the benches to my right. 'What happened to Master Lister were a tragedy, Gentlemen of the Jury, sure enough. But it were not a murder, and there were no witchcraft. I swear it.'

Roger Nowell, heretofore silent, spoke up. 'Yet after your deliverance from this court not three months since, you undertook to join a great assembly of witches at Malkin Tower in the County of Lancaster, did you not? As my examinations prove, you were identified not only by the young James Device, the son and grandson of witches, but also by Katherine Hewitt, better known as Mouldheels and an acknowledged witch in those parts.'

'Why have we not heard from them?' Altham asked.

'They have been committed to the Castle of

Lancaster also on charges of witchcraft, Your Honour, along with others who have confirmed the proceedings of that wicked assembly. I do, however, have records of my examinations of these witnesses as they pertain to Mistress Jennet Preston, which will prove my allegations, and which I have here.' He passed papers to the two judges. 'These examinations also show that at this gathering – or witches' Sabbat—'

He paused long enough for the words to have their full effect.

'Jennet Preston here did entreat her fellow witches to aid her in her aim to kill the Master Lister still living. Once the witches had agreed to assist her, they arranged to meet once more a year hence, at the home of Jennet Preston, at which juncture she departed in a flash upon her familiar, a white foal.'

The court erupted into noise, part shock, and – I were pleased to note – I recognised more than one voice denying the charges on my behalf.

'My thanks, Master Nowell,' Altham said once order had been restored, then he paused to read the papers, and nodded. 'You may read out these examinations in full for the benefit of the Gentlemen of the Jury.'

I stared at the floor as the statements of the examinations of James and Jennet Device, their mother Elizabeth, and Mouldheels were read out.

Damn her, I'd thought her a friend. The testimony followed the lines of Nowell's summary, but they were not the words of any of my ilk. They would never have used such words as dined, aforesaid, or confer; them words had been put into their mouths by gentry. I had to hope the jurymen had the sense to see it.

'My thanks, Master Nowell. It now falls to me to address the jury.' Altham cleared his throat and pursed his lips in thought.

'Gentlemen of the Jury, it is your solemn duty to observe the particular circumstances of this disturbing matter. Firstly, that Master Thomas Lister Senior was heard by more than one person to denounce the prisoner at the barre, one Jennet Preston, at the time of his death.

'But the conclusion is of more consequence than all the rest, that on Jennet Preston being brought to the dead corpse, it bled afresh. And after her deliverance in Lent, it was proved that she rode upon a white foal, and was present in the great assembly at Malkin Tower with the witches, to entreat and pray aid from them to kill Master Lister, now living, for that he had prosecuted against her.

'And against these people you may not expect direct evidence, since all their works are the works of darkness, and they are presently themselves committed to gaol, at the neighbouring County of Lancaster. Therefore I pray God direct your consciences.'

Finally, I were allowed to sit. I watched the jury as they chattered, knowing they held my life in their hands. My mind were blank, I had no more thought. Happen I would never have words again.

The court grew restless as the whispered conversation continued. These matters were normally decided in a matter of minutes. Hope seeped into my soul, did this mean they would deliver me once more?

At length, Altham banged his gavel and the head man of the jury stood to address him. My heart knocked hard in my chest as I prepared to hear my fate.

'Master Foreman, have you come to a conclusion?' Altham asked.

'We have not, Your Honour.'

'I see. Are your jury close to coming to a consensus?'

'I fear not, Your Honour.'

'In that case, I discharge you to the Grand Jury House to continue your deliberations. Master Sheriff, please prepare a new jury for the next case. That of a seminary priest, I believe.'

I stared as the sheriff ushered the jury away. What were happening? I searched frantically for William. He were making his way toward me, but my gaoler hauled me away from his reach. I were to wait back int' chapel.

Back in Purgatory.

* * *

I stayed there until it grew dark, praying for deliverance from this nightmare, but when the gaoler at last came for me, he took me not back to the court house, but back to the filthy, stinking and still crowded dungeon.

I were wrong, this were not Purgatory, this were Hell.

Chapter 9

28th July 1612

'We, the Gentlemen of the Jury of the Summer Assizes of the Castle of York do find Jennet Preston guilty of the felony and murder by witchcraft of Thomas Lister Esquire, contained in the indictment against her.'

I staggered at the man's words, and would have fallen if it were not for the bench behind me.

I sat, my manacled hands raised in fists to my forehead, and stared between my arms at the men who had been swayed by the younger Lister into condemning me.

A wave of noise roared over me and I didn't understand, then William had hold of me.

He were weeping.

Nay, my William were *sobbing*!

I'd never seen the like.

Then he were retreating, and I called out, 'No! William!'

I heard him call my name, saw him struggling, and realised both bailiff and sheriff were pulling him away from me. I were on me own again. 'William.' I had no idea if I spoke his name aloud or just within mesen, there were too much of a clamour to be sure.

I blinked and looked about me. The whole courtroom were on their feet – apart from me, the jurymen, and the four men at the judgement bench.

I heard my name called by a score of voices; nay, two score at least, and realised the doors had been thrown open to pass the news on to the people gathered outside. I saw my sister and her husband, and them who'd sent food and coin: Old Man Hodgeson, Peggy and Alf, Mary, Betty; and many more besides had come from Gisborne and neighbouring parishes to stand by me.

A hammering rose above the voices, over and over. It put me in mind of a stone mason carving a memorial, and presently that were all I could hear. Hammering nails into my coffin. Then a new thought struck me, would I even be provided with a coffin?

The noise ceased and I stared in disbelief as Sir James Altham reached over to retrieve a black cap from the bailiff, which he took a few moments to arrange upon his head until he were satisfied.

'Jennet Preston, you have been convicted of the wilful murder by witchcraft of Thomas Lister Esquire, late of Westby Hall near Gisborne in Craven, by a jury who, after examining your case with caution have, constrained by the force of evidence, pronounced you guilty.

'It only remains that I pronounce the judgement of the court against you by the King's authority, which is that you be taken to the place from whence you came and from thence, on the morrow, to the place of execution, there to be hanged by the neck until you are dead, and that your body be given to the surgeons of the City of York to be dissected and anatomised.

'May Almighty God have mercy upon your soul.'

It seemed I would have no need of a coffin.

I were led back to the dungeon in a stupor. I had truly believed they would acquit me once more; that they would see Lister's crusade for what it were. What were different this time? And then I had it. Roger Nowell. He'd always been a loud-mouthed Puritan, and hated any and all who saw life and faith different to him.

I gave a thought to young James Device and his family, Chattox, Mouldheels, and the score of others who were awaiting this court to arrive at the Castle of Lancaster next month. They would soon be following me to wherever and whatever came next. I realised I would soon know whether the old faith or the new had it right. Whether there were a Purgatory or not, whether the Eucharist truly did transform to the blood and body of Christ as we of the old faith believed. Christ! Would I meet him on the morrow? Would he be there to welcome me, save me from the horrors mankind wrought?

I shivered, I would find out soon enough. Unless he were persuaded by my Puritan accusers and it would be the Devil there to greet me. I smiled at the thought that if that were so, he would surely help me return and become the wicked fiend they believed me to be.

I would visit Thomas Lister once more in that case.

I were shoved into the stench of incarceration. At least I knew that this were the final time.

As my eyes grew used to the gloom, I tried to make out the faces of those who were still here with me. I recognised the pirate, a few of the men incarcerated for assault or murder, the priests, the other women accused of witchcraft. I couldn't see Maggie or Lizzie and my heart held hope that they'd been delivered from this hell.

Everyone were silent, lost in their own minds, no doubt, and I made my way over to John Wilson's corner. I were concerned that I had not been greeted with his cackle.

He were not there. Had the gaol fever taken him so fast? Or had he found another way to escape this torment?

I sat. I had but a few hours to make my peace with God before I made my final journey.

After we had been fed – nowt but day-old bread, a little cheese, and weak ale – the door were flung open.

A man entered, flanked by guards. He proceeded around the room, speaking to each inmate in turn. I realised who he were. The Chaplain of the Castle, come to tend to all of us sentenced to hang on the morrow.

I watched him make his slow approach to my corner, and glanced up as Father Greaves sat hissen beside me. I nodded to him, glad of his presence. How our time in this place had changed us!

It were my turn for Protestant tending. I watched the man's mouth move as he urged me to acknowledge and confess my crimes; as he described in detail the Hell that awaited me should I not acknowledge my sins.

'I have committed no sin, and no crime,' I repeated. 'I am innocent.'

'You have chosen a dangerous path, Mistress Preston. Your immortal soul is at risk should you go to your judgement impenitent. Please let me help you.'

'Should you wish to help me, be so kind as to allow me to spend a moment with my husband before I am taken from here.'

The man sighed, then nodded. 'I shall do what I can to make that pass, happen he may have more success in impressing upon you the imperative of repentance.'

'My thanks.'

The chaplain left, and Father Greaves took my hand. 'Should you wish to speak to me, my child?'

I smiled at him and nodded, then spoke. 'Forgive me, Father, for I have sinned.'

The chaplain prevailed, and the gaoler fetched me to the same room in which I had previously met with William, although my irons were not released on this occasion.

No matter. I hurried to my husband as best as I were able, and savoured the touch of his arms about me, the kiss to my crown, the tears that dripped into my hair.

After several moments, he pulled back. 'Jennet, my love,' he whispered.

I lifted my hands, awkward in their restraints, to place a finger to his lips. 'What's done is done,' I said. 'Let us not speak of it, but treasure this last time together.'

He kissed me. Long and lingering, and with a passion that had not dimmed throughout our marriage. I returned his fervour, but soon had to gasp for air as sobs threatened to take me over.

I held my hands out to him, and he grasped them, flinching when he saw the bent thumbs and the soreness the iron shackles had caused to my wrists.

'It's of no consequence, William. I have borne much worse, and still shall.'

He planted a kiss on the redness.

'William, please, the ring, take it, it should be with you.'

'Jennet no, you must wear it till the last!'

I shook my head. 'The gaoler or hangman would keep it for hissen. It should be with you.'

He hesitated, then enclosed it with his fingers and pulled. It did not move. My hands and fingers bore the traces of the years of hard work done since we'd wed, as well as the scars of the thumbikins. I smiled as he pulled harder, his frown creasing as the ring refused to encircle my knuckle.

'Happen I have an idea,' he said, reaching into his doublet to pull out a small package. ' 'Tis a little crushed now, but the taste should be unaffected.' He opened the rough linen pouch to show me a pie. No doubt bought from one of the street sellers who had flocked to York to take advantage of the crowds attending the Assizes. And the hangings.

He cracked open the pastry casing, popped some mutton into my mouth, and while I devoured it, he used its grease to ease my wedding ring from my finger, then pushed the thin band securely into his scrip.

'I still have the coin you refused to use for a bed,' he said. 'Would you not like a bed tonight?'

I shook my head. 'I shall not sleep tonight,' I said. 'But if you could use it to persuade the gaoler to reduce the weight of my irons tomorrow, I'd be grateful.'

He swallowed hard and nodded. I opened my mouth to indicate my need of more mutton, and he obliged.

'Tell me of the others,' I said. 'The priests, the pirate and some others are still within the dungeon, but what of John Wilson? And Maggie Thorne and Lizzie Nixon?'

William looked puzzled. 'I know not of Wilson, but I knew of your friendship with Maggie and Lizzie, and took pains to learn their fate.'

I wondered how much coin the gaoler had demanded for this information.

'They were granted the choice of deportation.'

I sighed and smiled; so they would not have to face York's Tyburn – the three-legged mare as the gallows were known.

'Where do they travel to?'

'I know not, love. There are ships awaiting prisoners and goods on the Ouse, but what their heading shall be once they pass through the Humber and to the open sea is anyone's guess. France or the Netherlands if Providence is with them. Spain or even the lands of the Moors should they be denied Fortune.'

I thought about the two women who had become friends in the reeking gloom of our gaol, now crowded into the hold of a ship, which I could not imagine to be any better. They would have no knowledge of which land they would next step foot upon, nor what awaited them there. They would have no kin, no friends to aid them, no home nor coin. They would not understand the folk's speech, and no bugger would understand theirs. They would be killed if they set foot upon English soil at any time within the next seven years.

They may have escaped the noose, but instead, they would likely have a lingering death amongst strangers. I weren't sure that were a better fate than the three-legged mare.

Chapter 10

29th July 1612

The blackness were becoming penetrable. The sun were coming up. My last dawning – and the last for everyone in here. As one, we stood and gathered together by the thin slits in the east wall beyond which lay the River Foss, the same river that had seeped persistently into this dark chamber throughout my time here. I lifted my foot and brought it down in a splash – just to feel the sensation of water.

I felt little else, only a silent chill which had not lifted since I'd understood the import of Altham's words. Happen every other bugger here felt the same coldness, as none had spoken for hours. None had berated my splash. None had pushed any other to better their own position ont' floor. None had done owt but face the incoming sun, hushed and lost in their own terrors.

The door slammed open. This time I did not flinch. None turned to face the incomer until, one by one, we were shackled and forced from the room.

When my turn came, I followed the gaoler, watching my own two feet follow him step by step, wondering how they were doing that? I weren't telling them to lift and move forward. I weren't walking to my doom. Not I.

Yet my feet took another pace and another. Then sunlight, and my feet stopped as I lifted my face to the dawn rays, what little there yet were reaching over the castle walls.

I kept my face turned heavenward as I were pushed into the back of a cart and forced to sit. Father Greaves were with me, another woman, and another half dozen men I had not yet spoken with. But it were too late now to begin friendships.

Two guards with swords at their belts and holding old, battered pistols, their matches smouldering in readiness, climbed into the cart and sat at the back, keeping their weapons ready to bear on us. More on horseback fell in behind.

'Walk on.'

The cart jolted as the horse strained and stepped forward.

We left the castle through the South Gate. The walls were crumbling, with green sprouts and buds of nature finding life within them. Whole castle were falling down.

Rumbling over the drawbridge, I caught my last glimpse of the River Foss. I were determined to note every sight, savour every moment of life still allotted to me.

The cart turned westward through the arched postern and followed the walls, Clifford's Tower looming high above us. I granted mesen a small smile. It should have been a magnificent sight, but after the old gaoler had removed the battlements and roof to sell for his own gain afore he were stopped, it looked poor, and tumbledown. It reflected the might of the City of York no more, only its greed.

I took great delight in the sight of a tree growing through a gap in the curtain wall, and the pile of stone it had displaced with the power of its determination to live. There were a lesson in that somewhere.

We trundled alongside overhanging houses of timber almost close enough to touch, until we passed an open area and I could see the tall spire of St Mary's to our right. I stared up at its length as the carthorse plodded along its deadly route, wondering if it truly did point the way to Heaven. Or were it *all* a lie?

That thought made the chill inside me grow ever colder.

Before long, the great River Ouse were before us. My last ever sight of that majestic flow of water. I stared downstream as we crossed the stone bridge, and realised that Maggie and Lizzie would be laden in the hold of one of the three-masted ships anchored there, soon to escape York by that passage. I raised my hands in a salute – an easier process today since the gaoler had honoured his bargain with William and used lighter manacles for this journey – and were struck on the temple by one of the guards.

I cursed, and struggled back to a sitting position, just in time to see the last glimmer of the morning sun reflect off the rippled river. Then it were gone.

The cart slowed as Micklegate rose past St Martin's-cum-Gregory's Church, the carter bellowing to the crowds walking to Knavesmire to move aside and grant us passage. Many did not. This were their day out and they would wring as much enjoyment as they could from each moment of Hanging Day. It only came about once every three months.

Their reply were to boo and hiss, and to throw cabbage leaves and the filth from the street at us. I bowed my head, and allowed mesen a small smile at the guards being pelted just as thoroughly as the condemned.

Near the brow of the hill, we passed out of the city. Micklegate Bar were too narrow to allow folk to walk alongside us and we enjoyed a brief moment of peace as we passed beneath it.

I stared behind us at the city walls and bar. It had been prettied up for the visit of King James not ten years before, yet already its limestone facing were falling away to reveal the gritstone behind. It were still imposing though, reaching up ower thirty foot high, so William once told me, years ago, before either of us had ever thought of setting out on a journey such as this.

I glared at its turrets and battlements, and in

particular the stone figure of the King, the biggest witch hunter in the land. Well, I would never again have to suffer the City of York, nor the rest of King James's England.

The road rose more shallowly as we proceeded along The Mount. Dwellings were replaced by green fields and woods, and I pulled in deep chestfuls of the sweet, country air. I closed my eyes, just for a moment, and imagined mesen to be at home, then flicked them open as a new, louder sound rolled around us. I could not imagine what it could be.

The cart turned past the Knavesmire herdsman's cottage and pinfold filled with his sheep, and I saw.

The large green swathe of land known as Knavesmire were full of people. With those I knew were still making their way here, there would be thousands of witnesses to this sham of justice.

Guards pushed people aside to make way for us, and the cart stopped. This were York's Tyburn. This then, were the three-legged mare.

Chapter 11

A trinity of upright wooden posts, nay, roughly carved tree trunks, stood in a patch of green. Two of the posts were connected by a high beam, and as I watched, a second were heaved up for the men on ladders to position into place and secure the joints. I winced at every hammer blow.

The cart came to a shuddering stop behind two others. I recognised some faces, but not all. Ours had not been the only dungeon of the damned then.

The third beam were dropped into place to finish and connect the lofty trio. As one we flinched with the thud of it, and then with each hammer blow securing the join.

I dragged my eyes away from the scaffold and scanned the crowd of people. My breath grew fast as I took in just how many people were here. How many people were enjoying this day.

My eyes lit on a pair of arms waving overhead. I recognised them sleeves. My sister had laboured near a year on the embroidery, despite being no seamstress. She had never worn them since she'd overheard Peggy Arkwright mock them, and my eyes teared as I realised she had worn them today to make sure I would see her.

I called her name as she approached but she were shoved backwards by the guards. They would not let her come close enough for private talk. No matter, it were good to know she were here. What were there left to say, anyroad? I searched again, trying to find William, but to no avail. Were this too much for him? Would he really allow me to face this without him?

The crowd made a loud, rising gasp and I turned back to the three-legged mare. More men, swathed with rope, climbed up the ladders to sit astride the crossbeams. I watched them knot nooses with a practised twirl before securing a number of them to each of the three beams.

It were now a gallows true.

A roar from the crowd went up, and I raised my head from my fearful prayers. A prisoner were being removed from a cart ahead and led to a smaller one with low bars. I recognised the pirate.

He did not make it easy for them to get him on to the cart, but there were little he could do to stop four men with pistol and cudgels from forcing him on to the platform, and he were soon curled up in a ball on the deck of his final vessel.

The groom clicked the horse to walk on and led the beast until the cart were positioned below the area where the crossbeams met the farthest post of the three-legged mare.

The pirate refused to stand, until two guards clambered up and hauled him to his feet.

The hangman placed the closest rope around his neck and slid the gallows knot to tighten the noose. Two men still sitting atop the crossbeam took up the slack and secured the rope before the guards made their way down from the cart.

They were replaced by a clergyman I didn't know. Presumably he were the incumbent of St Martin's – the closest church to Knavesmire.

The pirate stood with his back to the crowd, much to the evident annoyance of the clergyman, who kept pulling on the pirate's shoulder to turn him.

Once the reverend had finished his prayers, he were helped down and left the condemned man alone.

The hangman raised an arm, and the crowd hushed. The groom's words, 'Walk on,' were clear, and the horse moved forward, bringing the cart with it.

I held my breath, as I'm sure did most of the crowd, as the man scurried to the very back, then his feet scrabbled to keep some contact with the top rail of the cart.

He were soon left hanging.

His legs continued to kick a jig, to a roar of satisfaction of the crowd.

I wondered why no one had the decency to come forward and pull on the man's legs. It would hasten his end and relieve at least some of his suffering. Did he have no loved ones here?

Then I realised.

The guards were keeping all observers back.

None would be allowed through to ease the pain of hanging.

My legs shook, and I fell against Father Greaves with a sob.

He were praying, even as the next cart pulled into position next to the pirate's still twitching legs.

They were taking people from our cart now. I grabbed hold of Father Greaves' hand, desperate to stick together, mumbling our prayers, for ourselves and each other.

I thought back to our first meeting, and were so pleased I'd made the effort with the food William had brought to forge friendships in that place. I weren't sure I could face this without the Father's solid – although now diminished – presence.

Our grasp became tighter when the other woman – her name escapes me – were pulled away from the Father's other hand with a desperate cry. She were also to die as a witch.

I held the Father with both hands now, staring into his eyes, unable to watch any more folk die. The other men in the cart crowded around us – we were all together now – and the priest began a new prayer:

'By the authority which the Apostolic See has given me, I grant you a full pardon and the remission of all your sins in the name of the Father, and of the Son, and of the Holy Spirit.'

He thumbed a cross on my forehead, then the man next to me and the man next to him before the gaoler grabbed hold of the old priest and pulled him away.

'No!'

I doubled over at the pain in my chest and could not get my breath, then I heard a familiar voice call my name.

I glanced up and saw Lister. Saw the satisfaction on his face to see me so reduced.

I forced mesen to straighten, to breathe, to stand tall. To face what were coming. Lister looked away in disgust at my show of strength, and not before time.

Two crossbeams were laden with swinging bodies. Father Greaves were taken to the third.

I couldn't look. I couldn't watch him die.

My knees sagged once more at the command of, 'Walk on,' and I searched out my sister, tears running down both our faces.

'Master Gaoler, I demand the body of Mistress Jennet Preston for execution.'

I opened my eyes to see York's sheriff standing

before me, and heard my sister's protests, echoed by more friends and neighbours as I were taken to one of the small carts. I looked at the faces of them I knew, then my eyes found Katharine Dodgeson's. The mother of the baby boy Lister had tried and failed to convince Bromley I had murdered.

My heart pounded with hatred. Katharine Dodgeson were there when Old Lister died. She were at his laying out. She knew the truth, why did she not speak out? Then I saw Lister's hand on her husband's shoulder and understood. My hatred melted away. This were not her fault. Lister had taken advantage of her terrible loss. Used the death of poor little Thomas Dodgeson for his own ends.

I looked away, and at long last found William. Now I knew why I had not seen him beforehand. He must have been here through the night to ensure he had a place close by the scaffold. Close enough to keep my eyes on his as I were despatched. Close enough to pull on my legs to reduce the horror of my torment – if the guards would let him. He gave me a small smile and I almost broke.

The cart came to a halt by Father Greaves' legs and feet, and the hangman clambered on to the small platform. I gasped as I saw familiar features. 'John?' I croaked.

John Wilson didn't reply. He didn't even look me in the eye. So this were how he were paying his debt. By collecting on ours.

'John, please.'

He coloured and whispered, 'Sorry, lass,' as he placed the rope around my neck and pulled the knot tight.

I stared at him, then around in terror, searching for William's eyes once more.

Then a cleric were standing before me, offering me the host and a sip of wine. My lips moved of their own accord as I accepted my last Eucharist. Were this the body and blood of Christ? Or a mere approximation of it? I found it did not much matter anymore.

The cleric asked if I had anything to say, and I stared at him. 'I am no witch, and I have committed no crime.'

'Mistress, I beg you, please do not die impenitent, it would go ill for you.'

'I am innocent,' I repeated.

'God have mercy on your soul,' he said, then climbed down.

My eyes found William's for the last time, and locked there. He were all I were aware of now, all I wanted to be aware of.

'Walk on.'

The End

Murder by Witchcraft

Look out for more Pendle Witch short stories, coming soon. Join Karen's newsletter via her website to be notified of new releases, and receive an exclusive free Valkyrie short story, *Where Away*.

www.karenperkinsauthor.com

You are very welcome to join Karen in her Facebook group, to get the news about upcoming events and releases first, and to discuss and share your thoughts and/or questions about any of Karen's fiction:

www.facebook.com/groups/karenperkinsbookgroup

Acknowledgements

Thank you so much to the staff at York Castle Museum, particularly Martyn B, who helped me to build a mental picture of the 17th-century castle, dungeon and the conditions likely to have been faced by Jennet Preston in her incarcerations of 1612.

I am very grateful to my good friend and editor, Louise Burke – I rely on you to save my blushes and you never disappoint!

To family, friends and most importantly, thank you, Dear Reader. The posts, comments, messages and reviews you share with me, whether in person, on social media or online retailers lift me, motivate me, and are so very much appreciated. There is no better feeling for an author than to know people are willing and eager to read her books.

For more information on the full range of Karen Perkins' fiction, please visit Karen's website:
www.karenperkinsauthor.com

If you would like to find out more about the events that inspired this short story, the following books make for fascinating reading:

Almond PC (2012) *The Lancashire Witches: A Chronicle of Sorcery and Death on Pendle Hill,* I.B.Taurus, London

Borman T (2014) *Witches: James I and the English Witch-Hunts,* Vintage, Random House, London

Lumby J (1995) *The Lancashire Witch-Craze: Jennet Preston and the Lancashire Witches, 1612,* Carnegie Publishing Ltd, Lancaster

Poole R (2011) *The Wonderful Discovery of Witches in the County of Lancaster,* Palatine Books, Lancaster.

Trials, 1600-1926, Extraordinary Life and Character of Mary Bateman, the Yorkshire Witch, MOML, Monograph, Leeds

More Books by Karen Perkins

The Yorkshire Ghost Stories

Ghosts of Haworth
Parliament of Rooks: Haunting Brontë Country

Ghosts of Thores-Cross
The Haunting of Thores-Cross: A Yorkshire Ghost Story
Cursed: A Yorkshire Ghost Short Story
JENNET: now she wants the children

Ghosts of Knaresborough
Knight of Betrayal: A Medieval Haunting

The Haunting of Thores-Cross, Cursed, Knight of Betrayal and *Parliament of Rooks* are also available together in a box set at a reduced price:
Ghosts of Yorkshire

Karen Perkins

Pendle Witch Short Stories

Murder by Witchcraft
Divided by Witchcraft

The Valkyrie Series
Historical Caribbean Nautical Adventure

Look Sharpe! (Book #1)
Ill Wind (Book #2)
Dead Reckoning (Book #3)

*The Valkyrie Series: The First Fleet (Look Sharpe!,
Ill Wind & Dead Reckoning)*

About the Author

Karen Perkins is the author of the Yorkshire Ghost Stories, the Pendle Witch Short Stories and the Valkyrie Series of historical nautical fiction. All of her fiction has appeared at the top of bestseller lists on both sides of the Atlantic, including the top 21 in the UK Kindle Store in 2018.

Her first Yorkshire Ghost Story – THE HAUNTING OF THORES-CROSS – won the Silver Medal for European Fiction in the prestigious 2015 Independent Publisher Book Awards in New York, whilst her Valkyrie novel, DEAD RECKONING, was long-listed in the 2011 MSLEXIA novel competition.

Originally a financial advisor, a sailing injury left Karen with a chronic pain condition which she has been battling for over twenty five years (although she did take the European ladies title despite the injury!). Writing has given her a new lease of – and purpose to – life, and she is currently working on *A Question of Witchcraft* – a sequel to *Parliament of Rooks: Haunting Brontë Country,* as well as more Pendle Witch short stories.

KAREN PERKINS

To find out more about current writing projects as well as special offers and competitions, you are very welcome to join Karen in her Facebook group. This is an exclusive group where you can get the news first, as well as have access to early previews and chances to get your hands on new books before anyone else.
Find us on Facebook at:
www.facebook.com/groups/karenperkinsbookgroup

See more about Karen Perkins, including contact details and sign up to her newsletter, on her website:
www.karenperkinsauthor.com

Karen is on Social Media:

Facebook:
www.facebook.com/karenperkinsauthor
www.facebook.com/Yorkshireghosts
www.facebook.com/groups/karenperkinsbookgroup

Twitter:
@LionheartG

Instagram:
@yorkshireghosts

Lightning Source UK Ltd.
Milton Keynes UK
UKHW041833040721
386623UK00001B/7

9 781912 842384